THIS PLANNER BELONGS TO:

_____

CONTACTS

NAME	ADDRESS	NUMBERS

2021

JANUARY

SUN	MON	TUE	WED	THU	FRI	SAT
					1	2
3	4	5	6	7	8	9
10	11	12	13	14	15	16
17	18	19	20	21	22	23
24	25	26	27	28	29	30
31						

FEBRUARY

SUN	MON	TUE	WED	THU	FRI	SAT
	1	2	3	4	5	6
7	8	9	10	11	12	13
14	15	16	17	18	19	20
21	22	23	24	25	26	27
28						

MARCH

SUN	MON	TUE	WED	THU	FRI	SAT
	1	2	3	4	5	6
7	8	9	10	11	12	13
14	15	16	17	18	19	20
21	22	23	24	25	26	27
28	29	30	31			

APRIL

SUN	MON	TUE	WED	THU	FRI	SAT
				1	2	3
4	5	6	7	8	9	10
11	12	13	14	15	16	17
18	19	20	21	22	23	24
25	26	27	28	29	30	

MAY

SUN	MON	TUE	WED	THU	FRI	SAT
						1
2	3	4	5	6	7	8
9	10	11	12	13	14	15
16	17	18	19	20	21	22
23	24	25	26	27	28	29
30	31					

JUNE

SUN	MON	TUE	WED	THU	FRI	SAT
		1	2	3	4	5
6	7	8	9	10	11	12
13	14	15	16	17	18	19
20	21	22	23	24	25	26
27	28	29	30			

JULY

SUN	MON	TUE	WED	THU	FRI	SAT
				1	2	3
4	5	6	7	8	9	10
11	12	13	14	15	16	17
18	19	20	21	22	23	24
25	26	27	28	29	30	31

AUGUST

SUN	MON	TUE	WED	THU	FRI	SAT
1	2	3	4	5	6	7
8	9	10	11	12	13	14
15	16	17	18	19	20	21
22	23	24	25	26	27	28
29	30	31				

SEPTEMBER

SUN	MON	TUE	WED	THU	FRI	SAT
			1	2	3	4
5	6	7	8	9	10	11
12	13	14	15	16	17	18
19	20	21	22	23	24	25
26	27	28	29	30		

OCTOBER

SUN	MON	TUE	WED	THU	FRI	SAT
					1	2
3	4	5	6	7	8	9
10	11	12	13	14	15	16
17	18	19	20	21	22	23
24	25	26	27	28	29	30
31						

NOVEMBER

SUN	MON	TUE	WED	THU	FRI	SAT
	1	2	3	4	5	6
7	8	9	10	11	12	13
14	15	16	17	18	19	20
21	22	23	24	25	26	27
28	29	30				

DECEMBER

SUN	MON	TUE	WED	THU	FRI	SAT
			1	2	3	4
5	6	7	8	9	10	11
12	13	14	15	16	17	18
19	20	21	22	23	24	25
26	27	28	29	30	31	

IMPORTANT DATES

January 2021

SUNDAY	MONDAY	TUESDAY	WEDNESDAY
3	4	5	6
10	11	12	13
17	18 Martin Luther King, Jr. Day	19	20
24	25	26	27
31			

THURSDAY	FRIDAY	SATURDAY	NOTES
	1 New Year's Day	**2**	
	7	**8**	**9**	
	14	**15**	**16**	
	21	**22**	**23**	
	28	**29**	**30**	

February 2021

SUNDAY	MONDAY	TUESDAY	WEDNESDAY
	1	**2**	**3**
7	**8**	**9**	**10**
14 Valentine's Day	**15** Presidents' Day	**16**	**17** Ash Wednesday
21	**22**	**23**	**24**
28			

THURSDAY	FRIDAY	SATURDAY	NOTES
4	5	6	
11	12	13	
18	19	20	
25	26	27	

March 2021

SUNDAY	MONDAY	TUESDAY	WEDNESDAY
	1	2	3
7	8	9	10
14 Daylight Saving Time Begins	15	16	17 St. Patrick's Day
21	22	23	24
28 Palm Sunday	29	30	31

THURSDAY	FRIDAY	SATURDAY	NOTES
4	5	6	
11	12	13	
18	19	20 First Day of Spring	
25	26	27 Passover, Begins at Sunset	

April 2021

SUNDAY	MONDAY	TUESDAY	WEDNESDAY
4 Easter	**5**	**6**	**7**
11	**12**	**13**	**14**
18	**19**	**20**	**21**
25	**26**	**27**	**28**

THURSDAY	FRIDAY	SATURDAY	NOTES
1	**2** Good Friday	**3**	
8	**9**	**10**	
15	**16**	**17**	
22 Earth Day	**23**	**24**	
29	**30**		

May 2021

SUNDAY	MONDAY	TUESDAY	WEDNESDAY
2	3	4	5
9 Mother's Day	10	11	12
16	17	18	19
23	24	25	26
30	31 Memorial Day		

THURSDAY	FRIDAY	SATURDAY	NOTES
		1	
6	7	8	
13	14	15	
20	21	22	
27	28	29	

June 2021

SUNDAY	MONDAY	TUESDAY	WEDNESDAY
		1	2
6	7	8	9
13	14 Flag Day	15	16
20 Father's Day	21 First Day of Summer	22	23
27	28	29	30

THURSDAY	FRIDAY	SATURDAY	NOTES
3	4	5	
10	11	12	
17	18	19	
24	25	26	

July 2021

SUNDAY	MONDAY	TUESDAY	WEDNESDAY
4 Independence Day	**5**	**6**	**7**
11	**12**	**13**	**14**
18	**19**	**20**	**21**
25	**26**	**27**	**28**

THURSDAY	FRIDAY	SATURDAY	NOTES
1	2	3	
8	9	10	
15	16	17	
22	23	24	
29	30	31	

August 2021

SUNDAY	MONDAY	TUESDAY	WEDNESDAY
1	2	3	4
8	9	10	11
15	16	17	18
22	23	24	25
29	30	31	

THURSDAY	FRIDAY	SATURDAY	NOTES
5	6	7	
12	13	14	
19	20	21	
26	27	28	

September 2021

SUNDAY	MONDAY	TUESDAY	WEDNESDAY
			1
5	**6** Labor Day Rosh Hashanah, Begins at Sunset	**7**	**8**
12 Grandparents Day	**13**	**14**	**15** Yom Kippur, Begins at Sunset
19	**20**	**21**	**22** First Day of Autumn
26	**27**	**28**	**29**

THURSDAY	FRIDAY	SATURDAY	NOTES
2	3	4	
9	10	11 Patriot Day	
16	17	18	
23	24	25	
30			

October 2021

SUNDAY	MONDAY	TUESDAY	WEDNESDAY
3	4	5	6
10	11 Columbus Day	12	13
17	18	19	20
24	25	26	27
31 Halloween			

THURSDAY	FRIDAY	SATURDAY	NOTES
	1	2	
7	8	9	
14	15	16	
21	22	23	
28	29	30	

November 2021

SUNDAY	MONDAY	TUESDAY	WEDNESDAY
	1	**2** Election Day	**3**
7 Daylight Saving Time Ends	**8**	**9**	**10**
14	**15**	**16**	**17**
21	**22**	**23**	**24**
28 Hanukkah, Begins at Sunset	**29**	**30**	

THURSDAY	FRIDAY	SATURDAY	NOTES
4	**5**	**6**	
11 Veterans Day	**12**	**13**	
18	**19**	**20**	
25 Thanksgiving Day	**26**	**27**	

December 2021

SUNDAY	MONDAY	TUESDAY	WEDNESDAY
			1
5	6	7	8
12	13	14	15
19	20	21 First Day of Winter	22
26 Kwanzaa Begins	27	28	29

THURSDAY	FRIDAY	SATURDAY	NOTES
2	3	4	
9	10	11	
16	17	18	
23	24	25 Christmas Day	
30	31 New Year's Eve		

NOTES

NOTES

NOTES

NOTES

2022

JANUARY

SUN	MON	TUE	WED	THU	FRI	SAT
						1
2	3	4	5	6	7	8
9	10	11	12	13	14	15
16	17	18	19	20	21	22
23	24	25	26	27	28	29
30	31					

FEBRUARY

SUN	MON	TUE	WED	THU	FRI	SAT
		1	2	3	4	5
6	7	8	9	10	11	12
13	14	15	16	17	18	19
20	21	22	23	24	25	26
27	28					

MARCH

SUN	MON	TUE	WED	THU	FRI	SAT
		1	2	3	4	5
6	7	8	9	10	11	12
13	14	15	16	17	18	19
20	21	22	23	24	25	26
27	28	29	30	31		

APRIL

SUN	MON	TUE	WED	THU	FRI	SAT
					1	2
3	4	5	6	7	8	9
10	11	12	13	14	15	16
17	18	19	20	21	22	23
24	25	26	27	28	29	30

MAY

SUN	MON	TUE	WED	THU	FRI	SAT
1	2	3	4	5	6	7
8	9	10	11	12	13	14
15	16	17	18	19	20	21
22	23	24	25	26	27	28
29	30	31				

JUNE

SUN	MON	TUE	WED	THU	FRI	SAT
			1	2	3	4
5	6	7	8	9	10	11
12	13	14	15	16	17	18
19	20	21	22	23	24	25
26	27	28	29	30		

JULY

SUN	MON	TUE	WED	THU	FRI	SAT
					1	2
3	4	5	6	7	8	9
10	11	12	13	14	15	16
17	18	19	20	21	22	23
24	25	26	27	28	29	30
31						

AUGUST

SUN	MON	TUE	WED	THU	FRI	SAT
	1	2	3	4	5	6
7	8	9	10	11	12	13
14	15	16	17	18	19	20
21	22	23	24	25	26	27
28	29	30	31			

SEPTEMBER

SUN	MON	TUE	WED	THU	FRI	SAT
				1	2	3
4	5	6	7	8	9	10
11	12	13	14	15	16	17
18	19	20	21	22	23	24
25	26	27	28	29	30	

OCTOBER

SUN	MON	TUE	WED	THU	FRI	SAT
						1
2	3	4	5	6	7	8
9	10	11	12	13	14	15
16	17	18	19	20	21	22
23	24	25	26	27	28	29
30	31					

NOVEMBER

SUN	MON	TUE	WED	THU	FRI	SAT
		1	2	3	4	5
6	7	8	9	10	11	12
13	14	15	16	17	18	19
20	21	22	23	24	25	26
27	28	29	30			

DECEMBER

SUN	MON	TUE	WED	THU	FRI	SAT
				1	2	3
4	5	6	7	8	9	10
11	12	13	14	15	16	17
18	19	20	21	22	23	24
25	26	27	28	29	30	31

IMPORTANT DATES

January 2022

SUNDAY	MONDAY	TUESDAY	WEDNESDAY
2	3	4	5
9	10	11	12
16	17 Martin Luther King, Jr. Day	18	19
23	24	25	26
30	31		

THURSDAY	FRIDAY	SATURDAY	NOTES
		1 New Year's Day	
6	**7**	**8**	
13	**14**	**15**	
20	**21**	**22**	
27	**28**	**29**	

February 2022

SUNDAY	MONDAY	TUESDAY	WEDNESDAY
		1	2
6	7	8	9
13	14 Valentine's Day	15	16
20	21 Presidents' Day	22	23
27	28		

THURSDAY	FRIDAY	SATURDAY	NOTES
3	4	5	
10	11	12	
17	18	19	
24	25	26	

March 2022

SUNDAY	MONDAY	TUESDAY	WEDNESDAY
		1	2 Ash Wednesday
6	7	8	9
13 Daylight Saving Time Begins	14	15	16
20 First Day of Spring	21	22	23
27	28	29	30

THURSDAY	FRIDAY	SATURDAY	NOTES
3	4	5	
10	11	12	
17 St. Patrick's Day	18	19	
24	25	26	
31			

April 2022

SUNDAY	MONDAY	TUESDAY	WEDNESDAY
3	4	5	6
10 Palm Sunday	11	12	13
17 Easter	18	19	20
24	25	26	27

THURSDAY	FRIDAY	SATURDAY	NOTES
	1	**2**	
7	**8**	**9**	
14	**15** Good Friday Passover, Begins at Sunset	**16**	
21	**22** Earth Day	**23**	
28	**29**	**30**	

May 2022

SUNDAY	MONDAY	TUESDAY	WEDNESDAY
1	2	3	4
8 Mother's Day	9	10	11
15	16	17	18
22	23	24	25
29	30 Memorial Day	31	

THURSDAY	FRIDAY	SATURDAY	NOTES
5	6	7	
12	13	14	
19	20	21	
26	27	28	

June 2022

SUNDAY	MONDAY	TUESDAY	WEDNESDAY
			1
5	**6**	**7**	**8**
12	**13**	**14** Flag Day	**15**
19 Father's Day	**20**	**21** First Day of Summer	**22**
26	**27**	**28**	**29**

THURSDAY	FRIDAY	SATURDAY	NOTES
2	3	4	
9	10	11	
16	17	18	
23	24	25	
30			

July 2022

SUNDAY	MONDAY	TUESDAY	WEDNESDAY
3	4 Independence Day	5	6
10	11	12	13
17	18	19	20
24	25	26	27
31			

THURSDAY	FRIDAY	SATURDAY	NOTES
	1	2	
7	8	9	
14	15	16	
21	22	23	
28	29	30	

August 2022

SUNDAY	MONDAY	TUESDAY	WEDNESDAY
	1	2	3
7	8	9	10
14	15	16	17
21	22	23	24
28	29	30	31

THURSDAY	FRIDAY	SATURDAY	NOTES
4	5	6	
11	12	13	
18	19	20	
25	26	27	

September 2022

SUNDAY	MONDAY	TUESDAY	WEDNESDAY
4	**5** Labor Day	**6**	**7**
11 Grandparents Day Patriot Day	**12**	**13**	**14**
18	**19**	**20**	**21**
25 Rosh Hashanah, Begins at Sunset	**26**	**27**	**28**

THURSDAY	FRIDAY	SATURDAY	NOTES
1	2	3	
8	9	10	
15	16	17	
22	23 First Day of Autumn	24	
29	30		

October 2022

SUNDAY	MONDAY	TUESDAY	WEDNESDAY
2	3	4 Yom Kippur, Begins at Sunset	5
9	10 Columbus Day	11	12
16	17	18	19
23	24	25	26
30	31 Halloween		

THURSDAY	FRIDAY	SATURDAY	NOTES
		1	
6	7	8	
13	14	15	
20	21	22	
27	28	29	

November 2022

SUNDAY	MONDAY	TUESDAY	WEDNESDAY
		1	**2**
6 Daylight Saving Time Ends	**7**	**8** Election Day	**9**
13	**14**	**15**	**16**
20	**21**	**22**	**23**
27	**28**	**29**	**30**

THURSDAY	FRIDAY	SATURDAY	NOTES
3	**4**	**5**	
10	**11** Veterans Day	**12**	
17	**18**	**19**	
24 Thanksgiving Day	**25**	**26**	

December 2022

SUNDAY	MONDAY	TUESDAY	WEDNESDAY
4	**5**	**6**	**7**
11	**12**	**13**	**14**
18 Hanukkah, Begins at Sunset	**19**	**20**	**21** First Day of Winter
25 Christmas Day	**26** Kwanzaa Begins	**27**	**28**

THURSDAY	FRIDAY	SATURDAY	NOTES
1	**2**	**3**	
8	**9**	**10**	
15	**16**	**17**	
22	**23**	**24**	
29	**30**	**31** New Year's Eve	

NOTES

NOTES

2023

JANUARY

SUN	MON	TUE	WED	THU	FRI	SAT
1	2	3	4	5	6	7
8	9	10	11	12	13	14
15	16	17	18	19	20	21
22	23	24	25	26	27	28
29	30	31				

FEBRUARY

SUN	MON	TUE	WED	THU	FRI	SAT
			1	2	3	4
5	6	7	8	9	10	11
12	13	14	15	16	17	18
19	20	21	22	23	24	25
26	27	28				

MARCH

SUN	MON	TUE	WED	THU	FRI	SAT
			1	2	3	4
5	6	7	8	9	10	11
12	13	14	15	16	17	18
19	20	21	22	23	24	25
26	27	28	29	30	31	

APRIL

SUN	MON	TUE	WED	THU	FRI	SAT
						1
2	3	4	5	6	7	8
9	10	11	12	13	14	15
16	17	18	19	20	21	22
23	24	25	26	27	28	29
30						

MAY

SUN	MON	TUE	WED	THU	FRI	SAT
	1	2	3	4	5	6
7	8	9	10	11	12	13
14	15	16	17	18	19	20
21	22	23	24	25	26	27
28	29	30	31			

JUNE

SUN	MON	TUE	WED	THU	FRI	SAT
				1	2	3
4	5	6	7	8	9	10
11	12	13	14	15	16	17
18	19	20	21	22	23	24
25	26	27	28	29	30	

JULY

SUN	MON	TUE	WED	THU	FRI	SAT
						1
2	3	4	5	6	7	8
9	10	11	12	13	14	15
16	17	18	19	20	21	22
23	24	25	26	27	28	29
30	31					

AUGUST

SUN	MON	TUE	WED	THU	FRI	SAT
		1	2	3	4	5
6	7	8	9	10	11	12
13	14	15	16	17	18	19
20	21	22	23	24	25	26
27	28	29	30	31		

SEPTEMBER

SUN	MON	TUE	WED	THU	FRI	SAT
					1	2
3	4	5	6	7	8	9
10	11	12	13	14	15	16
17	18	19	20	21	22	23
24	25	26	27	28	29	30

OCTOBER

SUN	MON	TUE	WED	THU	FRI	SAT
1	2	3	4	5	6	7
8	9	10	11	12	13	14
15	16	17	18	19	20	21
22	23	24	25	26	27	28
29	30	31				

NOVEMBER

SUN	MON	TUE	WED	THU	FRI	SAT
			1	2	3	4
5	6	7	8	9	10	11
12	13	14	15	16	17	18
19	20	21	22	23	24	25
26	27	28	29	30		

DECEMBER

SUN	MON	TUE	WED	THU	FRI	SAT
					1	2
3	4	5	6	7	8	9
10	11	12	13	14	15	16
17	18	19	20	21	22	23
24	25	26	27	28	29	30
31						

CPSIA information can be obtained
at www.ICGtesting.com
Printed in the USA
BVHW051951130121
597730BV00009B/836

9 781648 421297